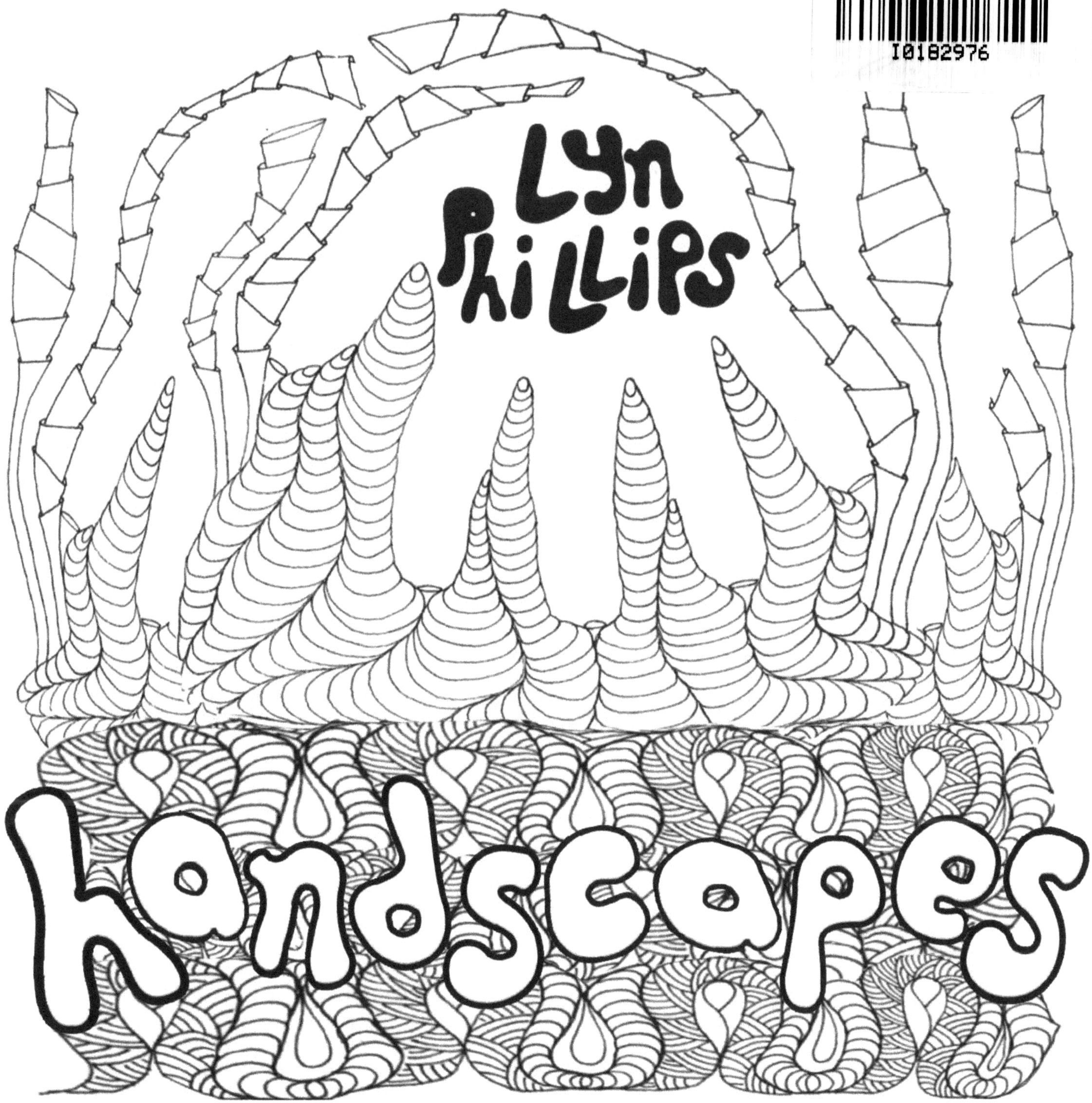
Lyn
Phillips
handscapes

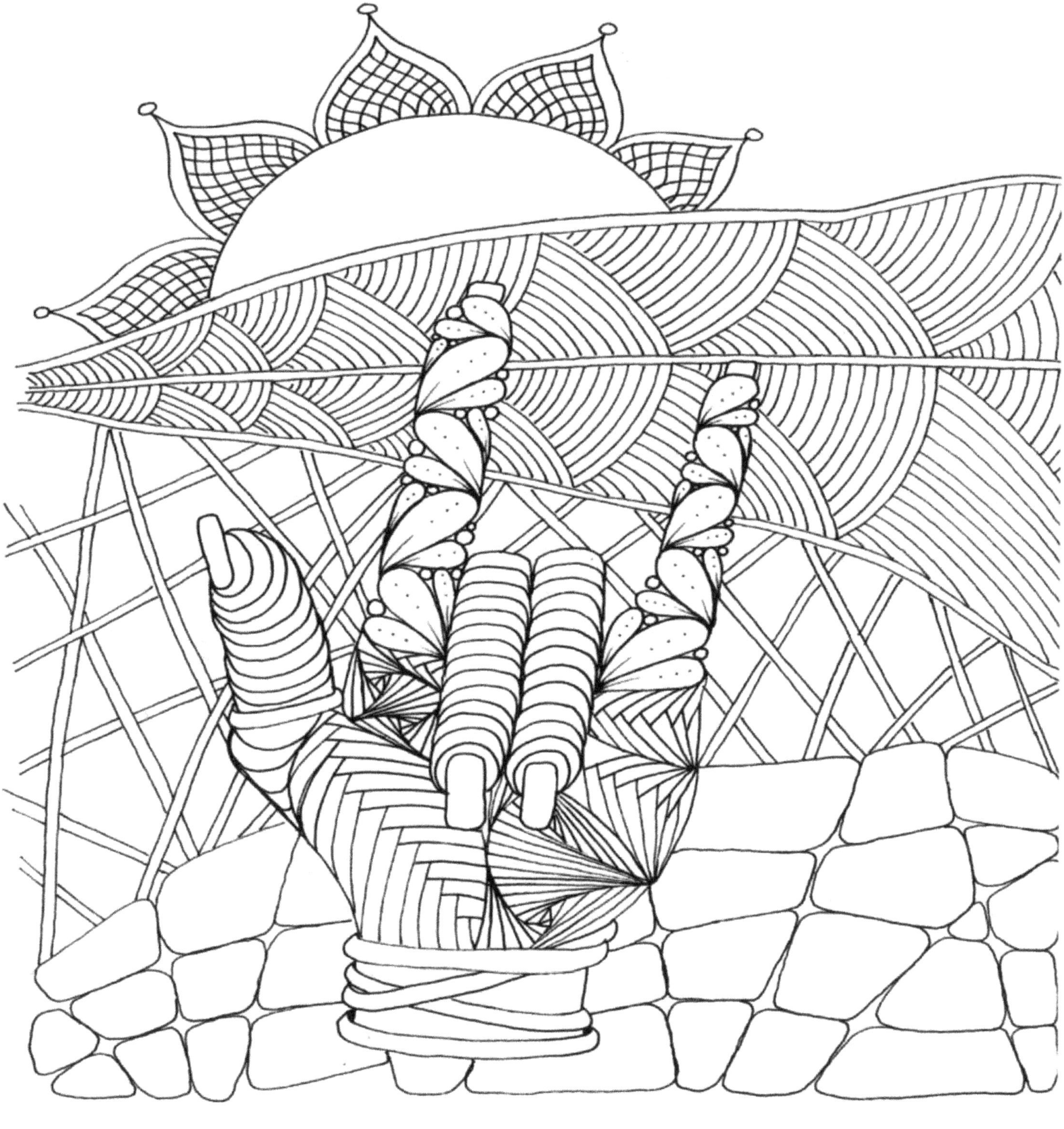

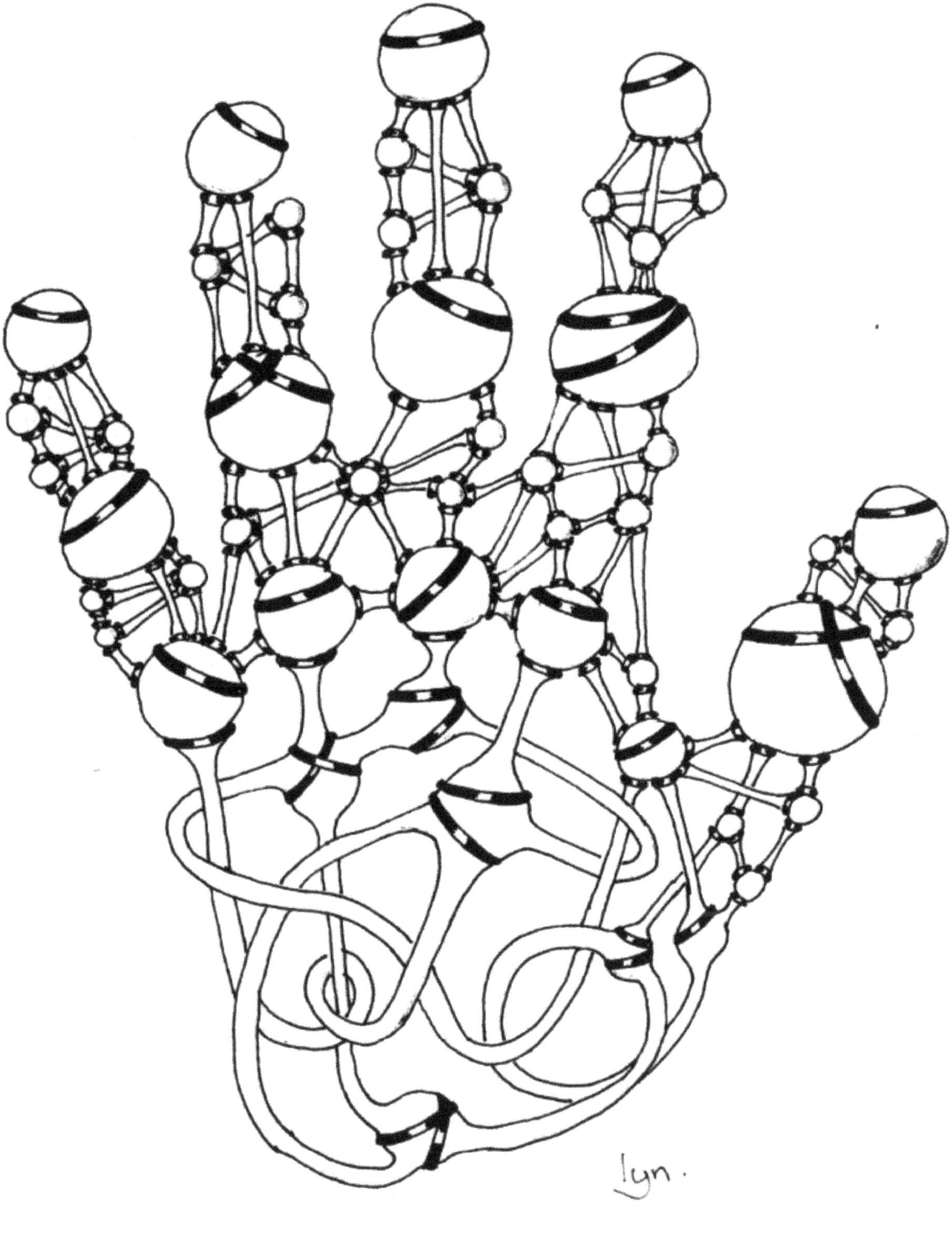
Lyn.

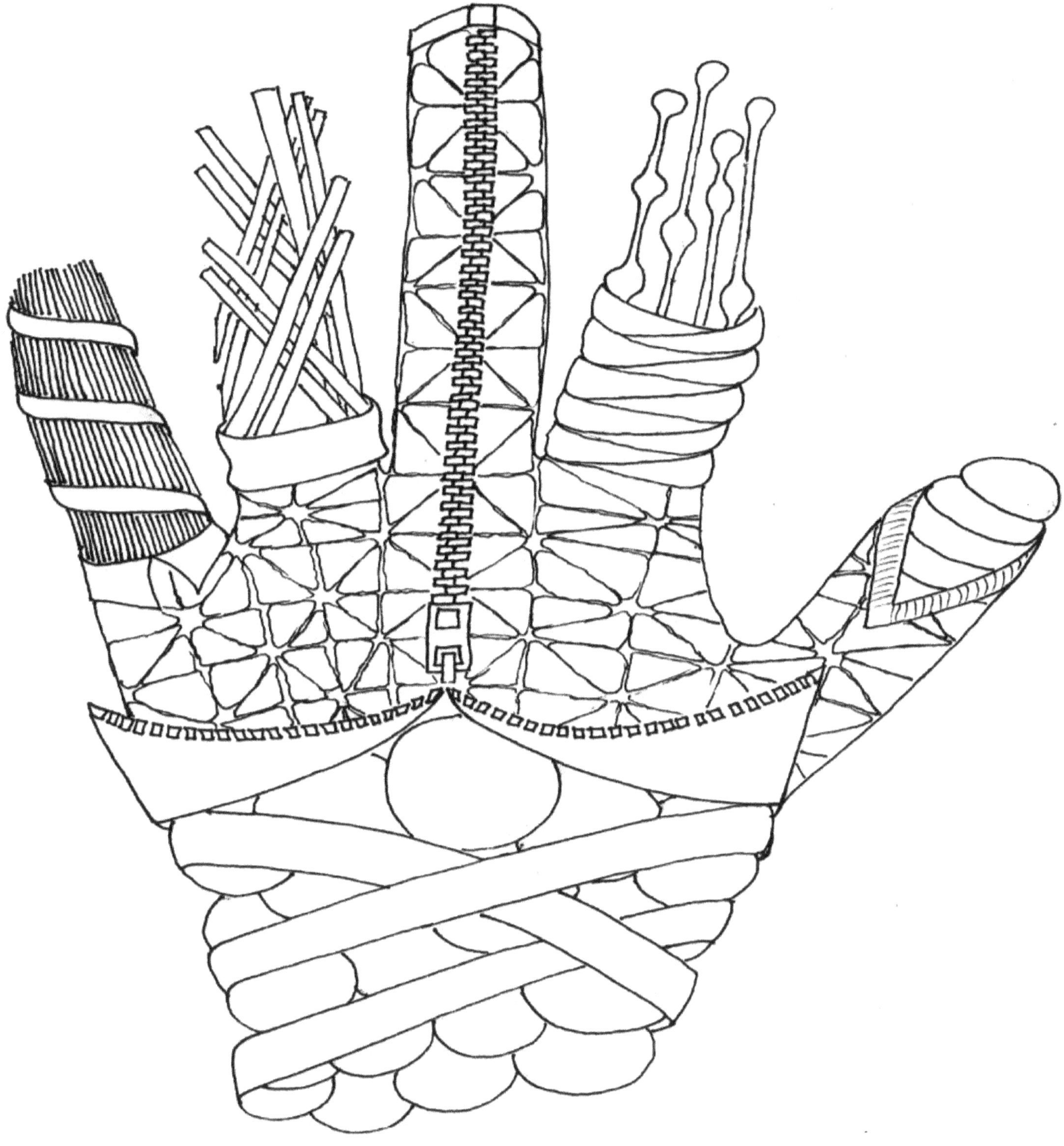

Lyn.

lyn.

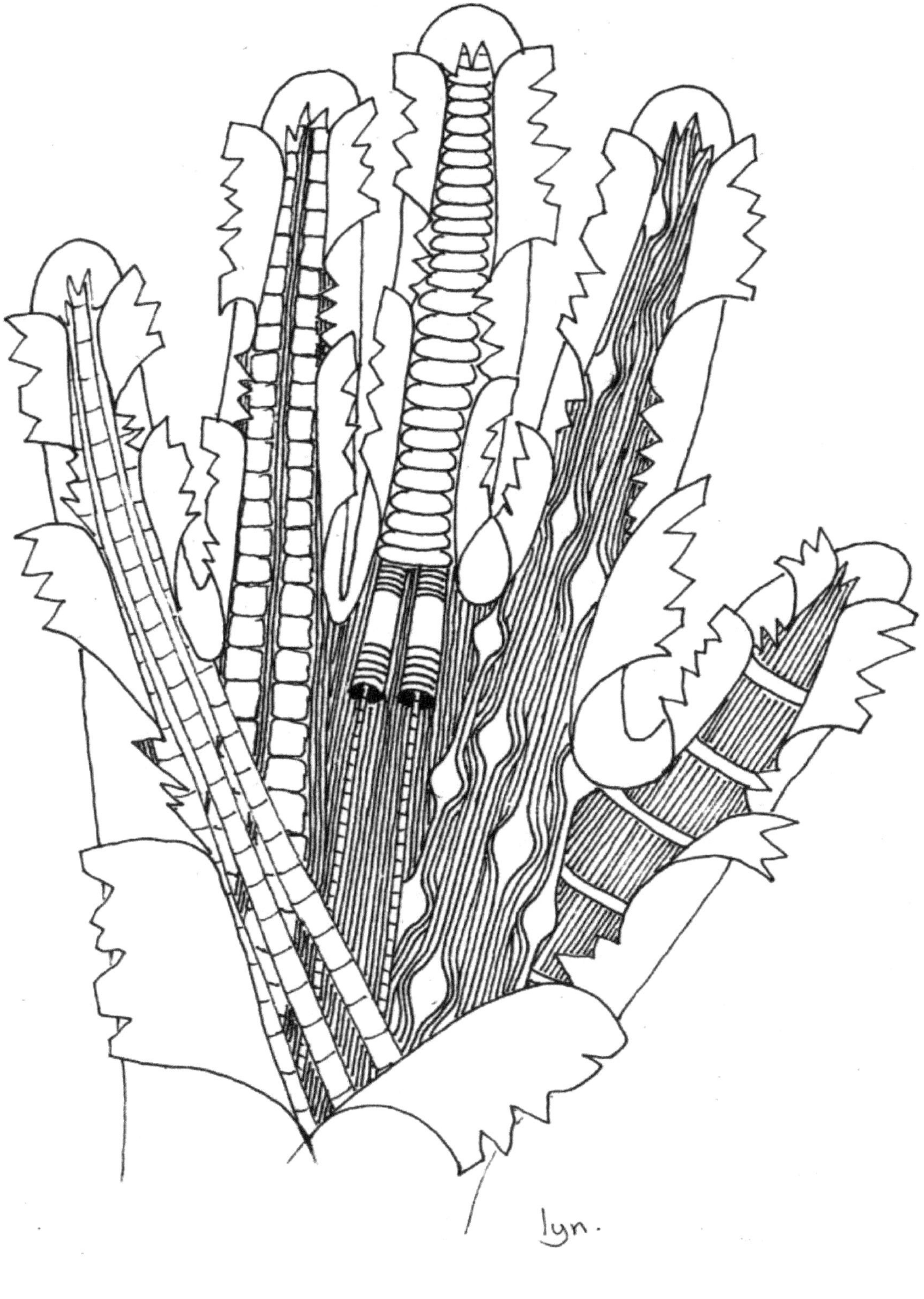
lyn.

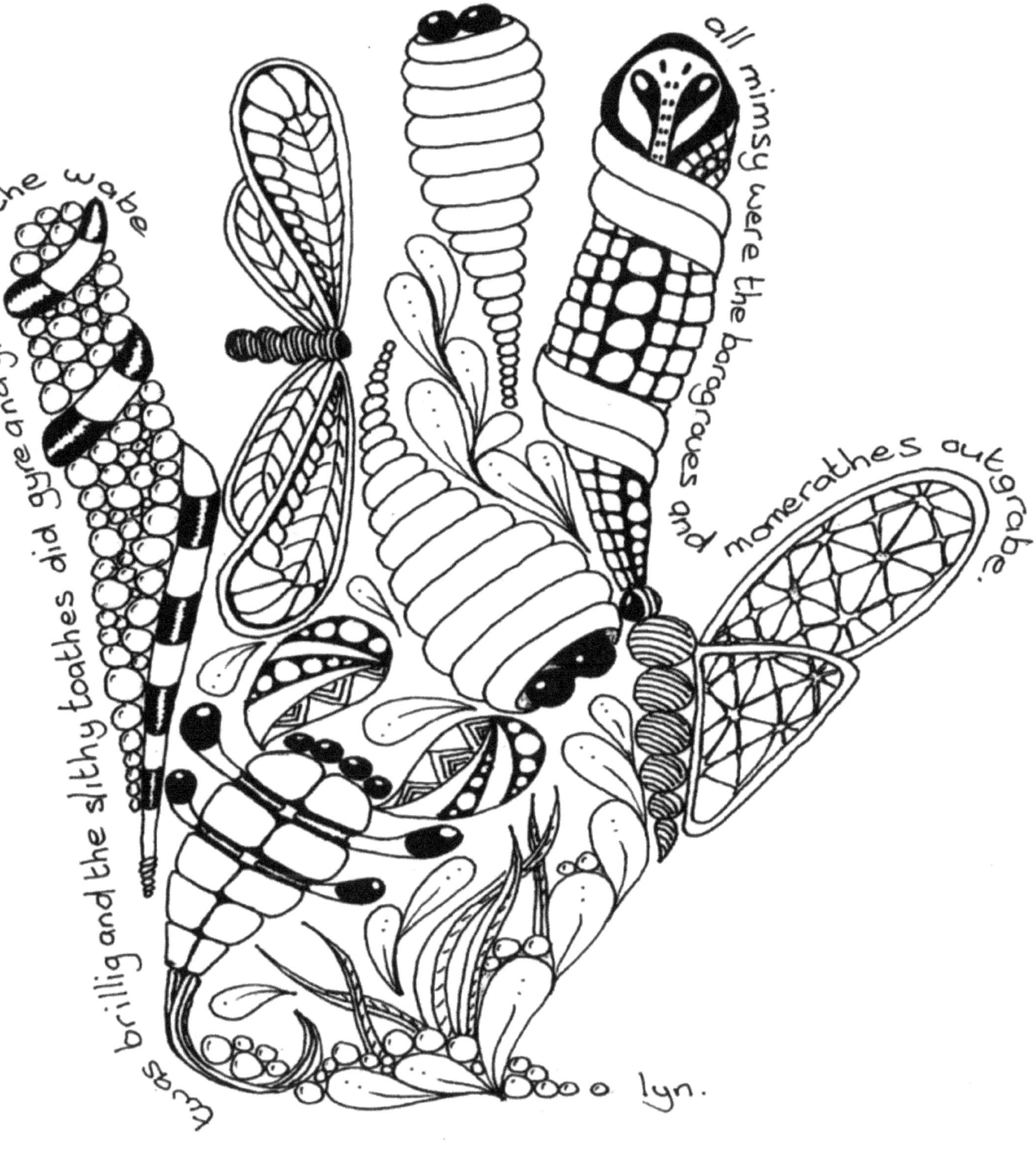
twas brillig and the slithy toathes did gyre and gimbal in the wabe
all mimsy were the boragraves and
momerathes outgrabe.
lyn.

lyn.

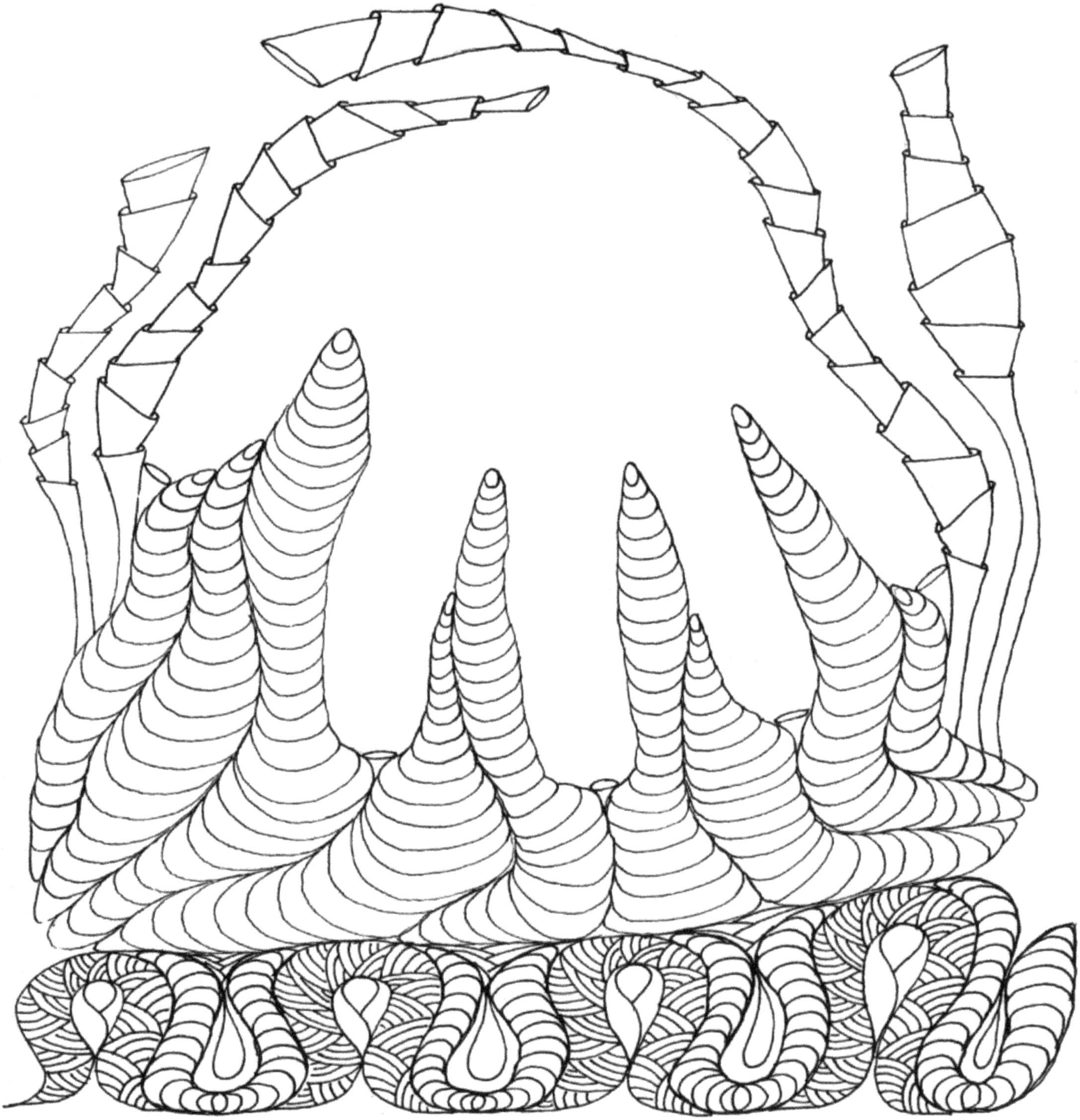

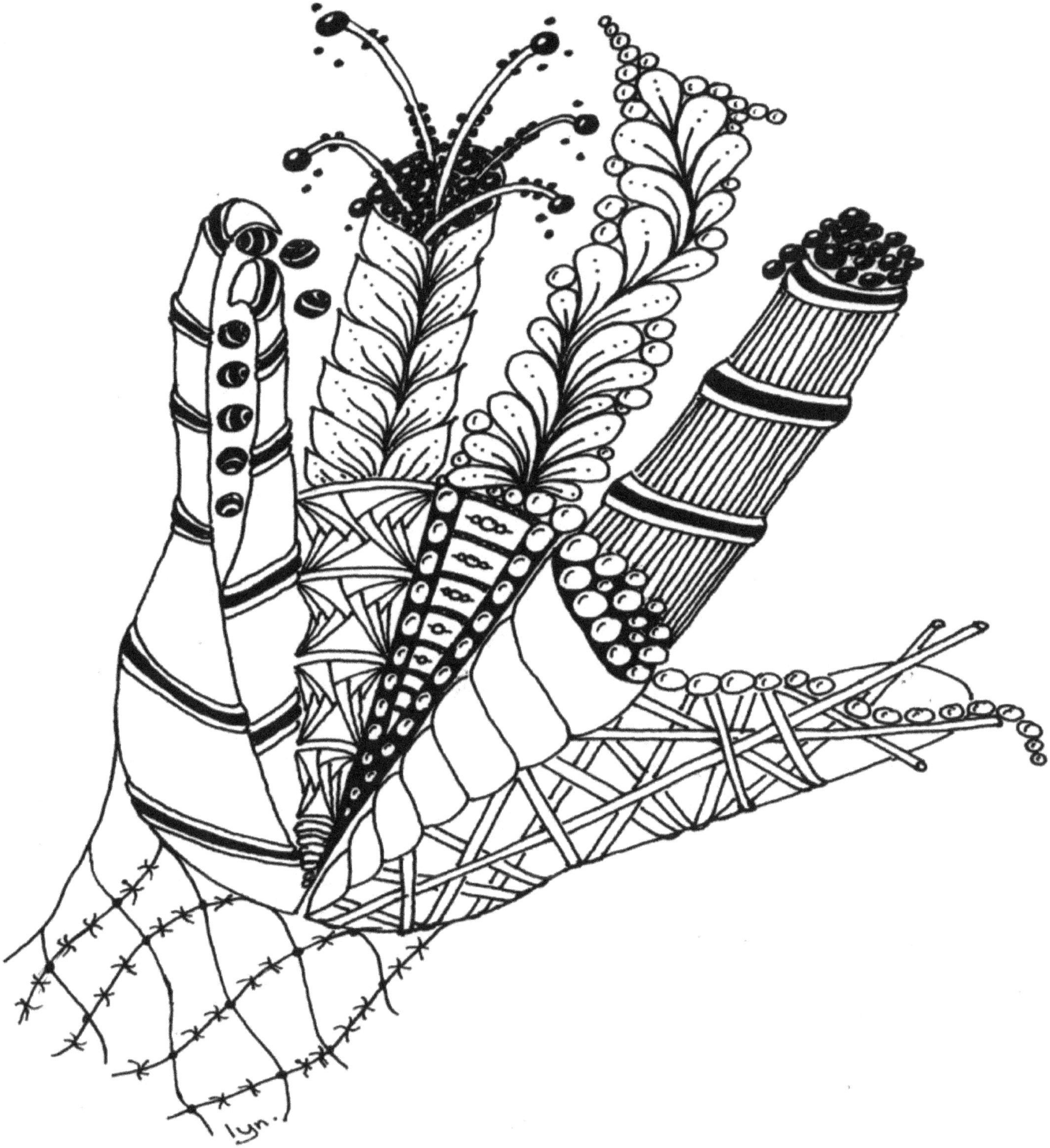
lyn.

lyn.

lyn.

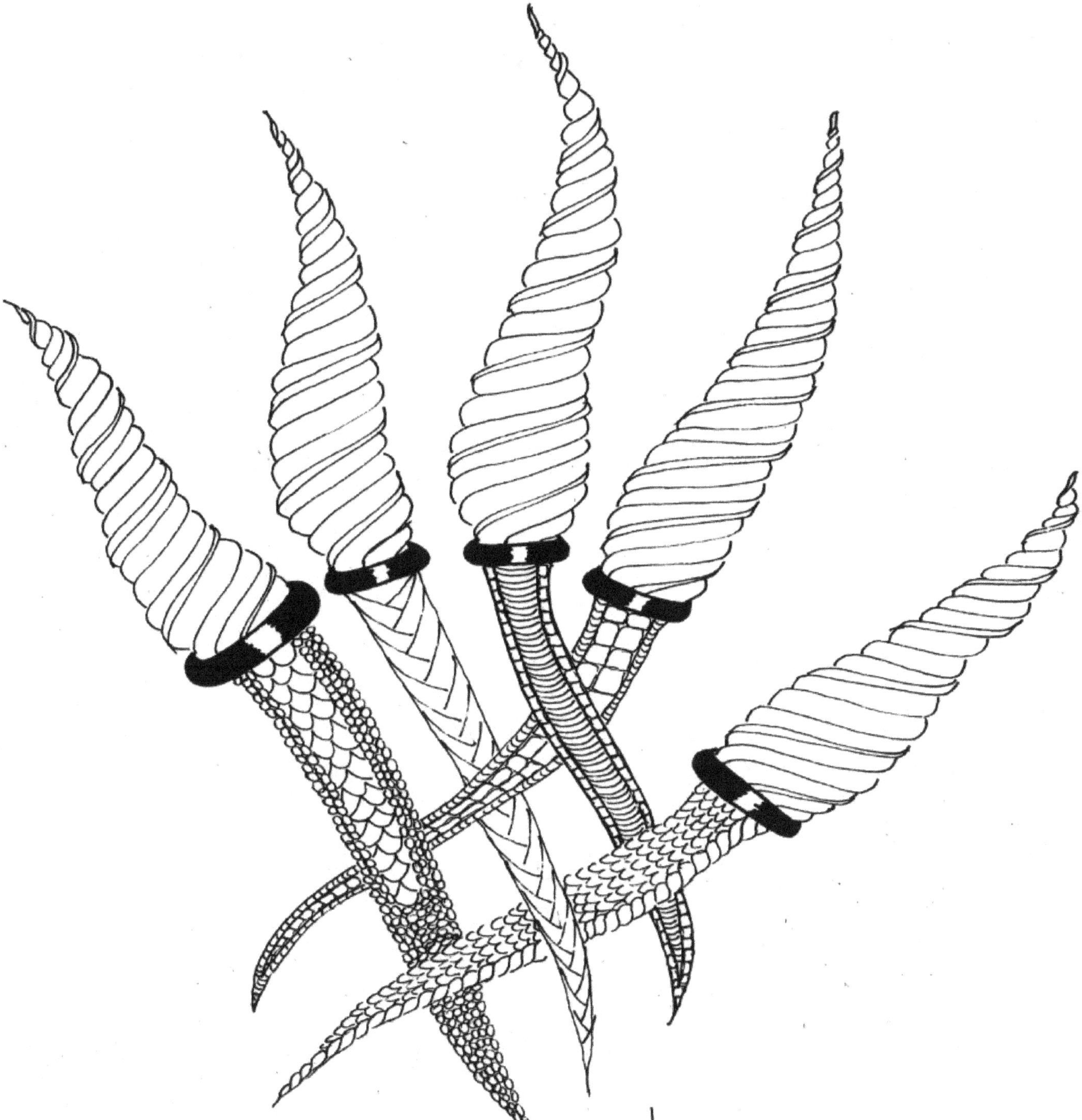
lyn.

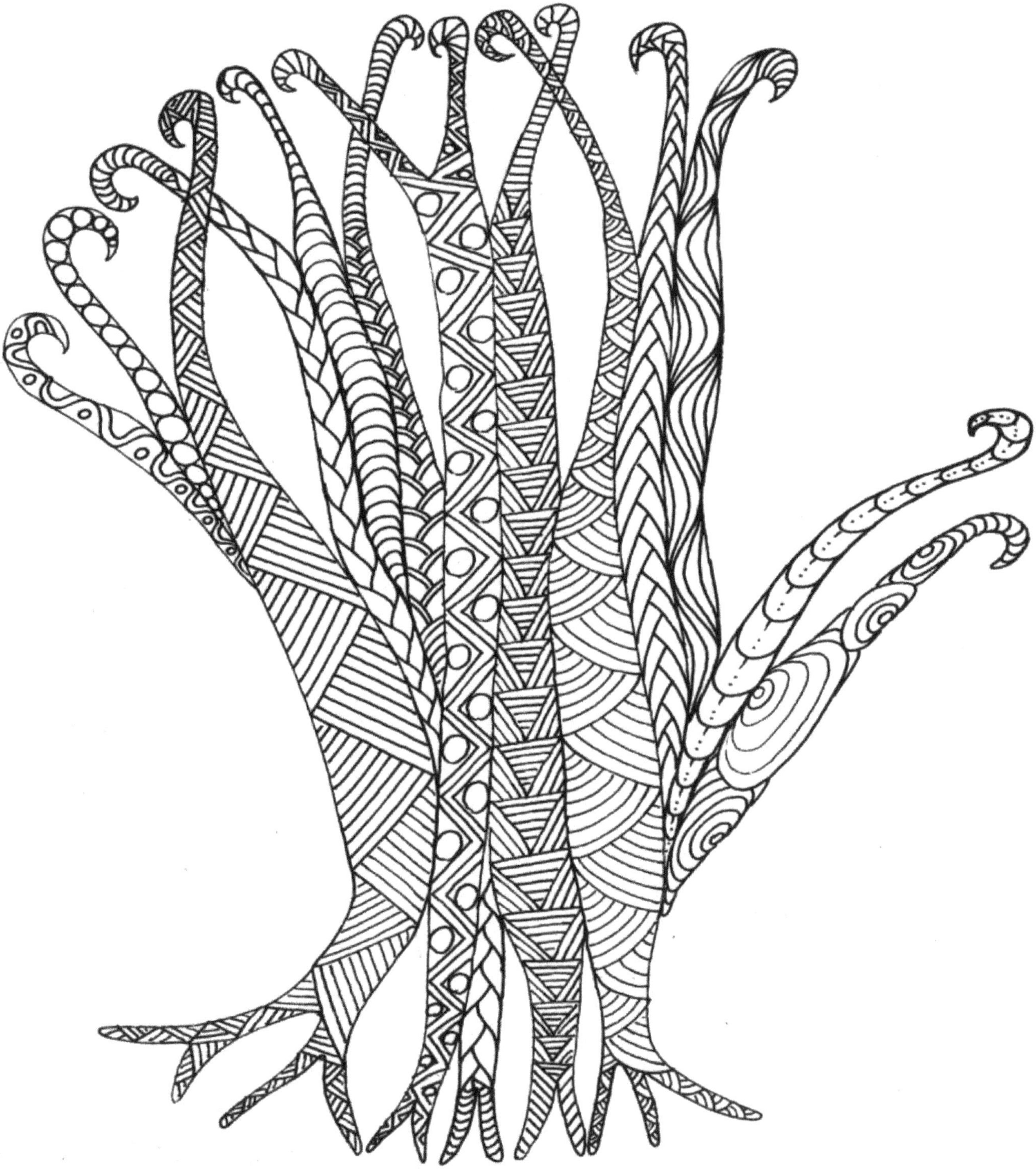

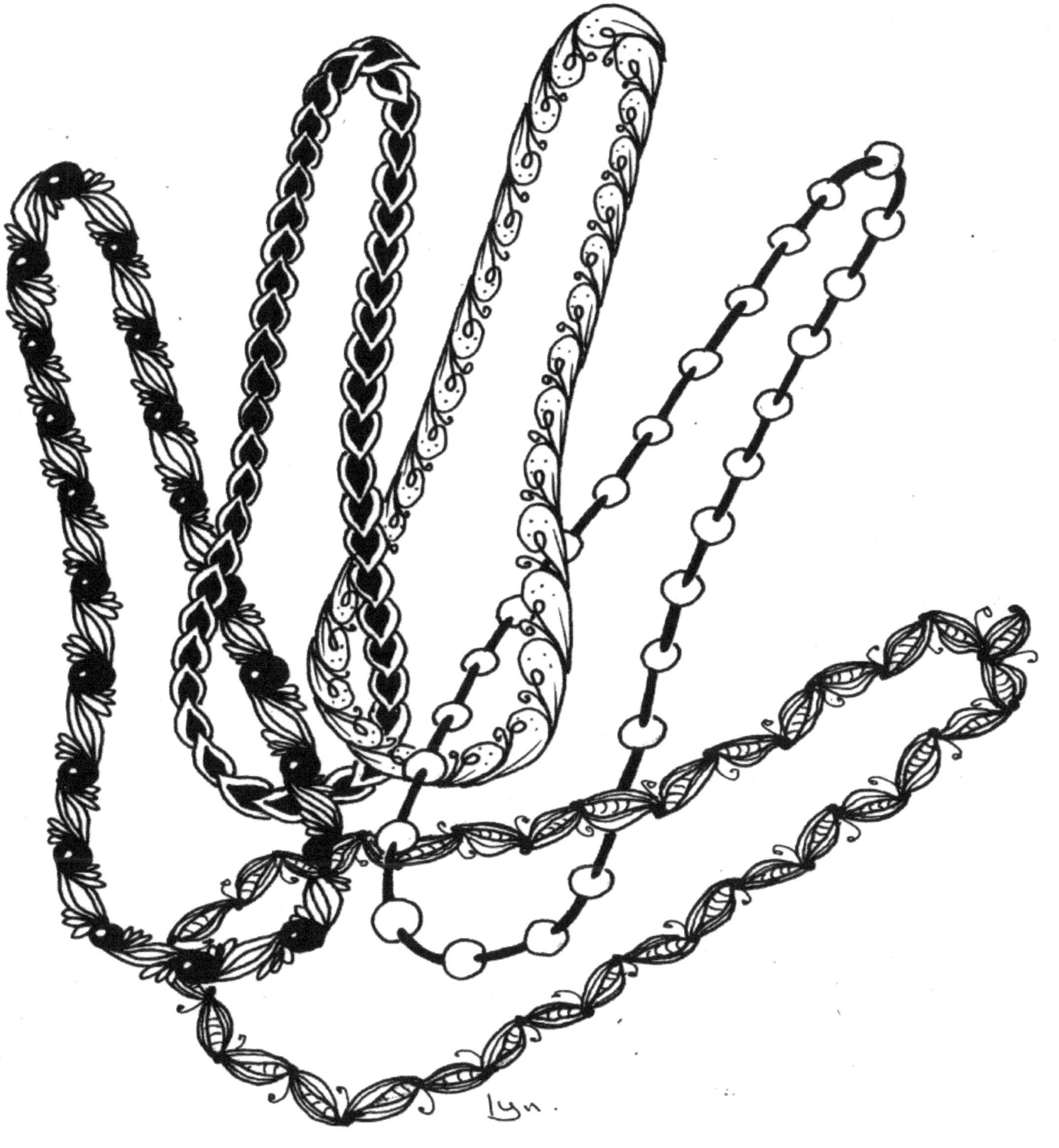
Lyn.

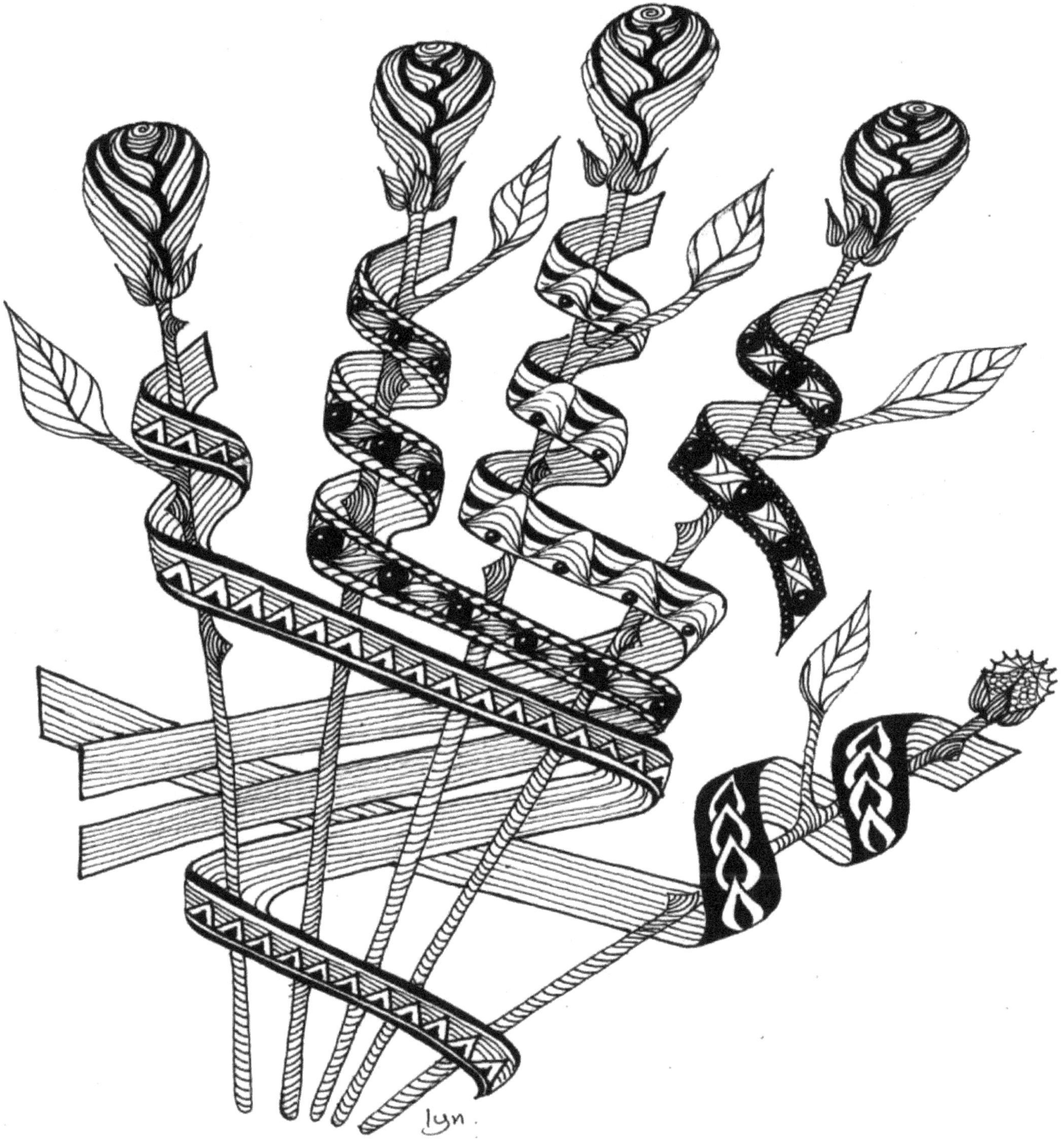
lyn

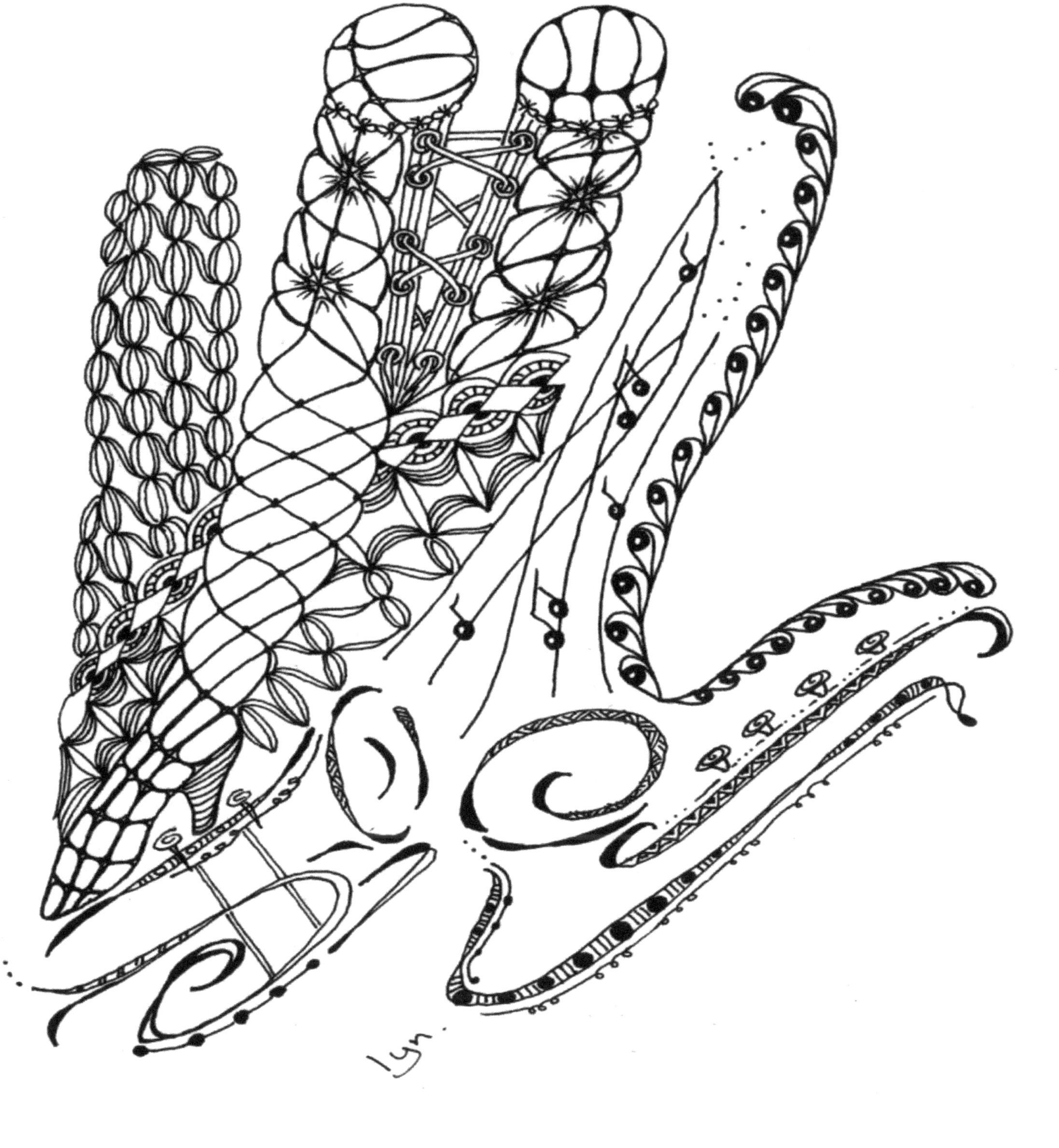

lyn.

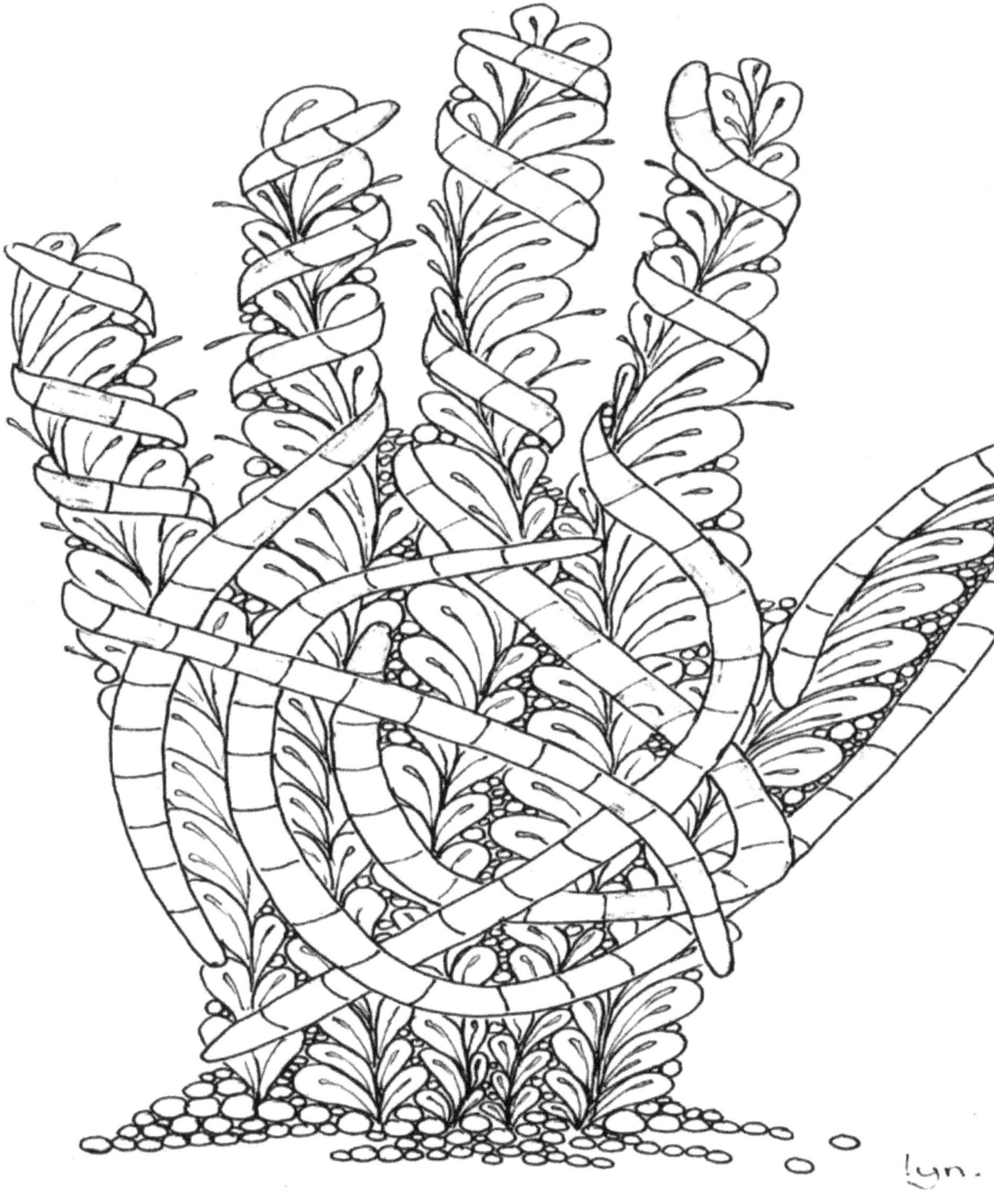
Lyn.

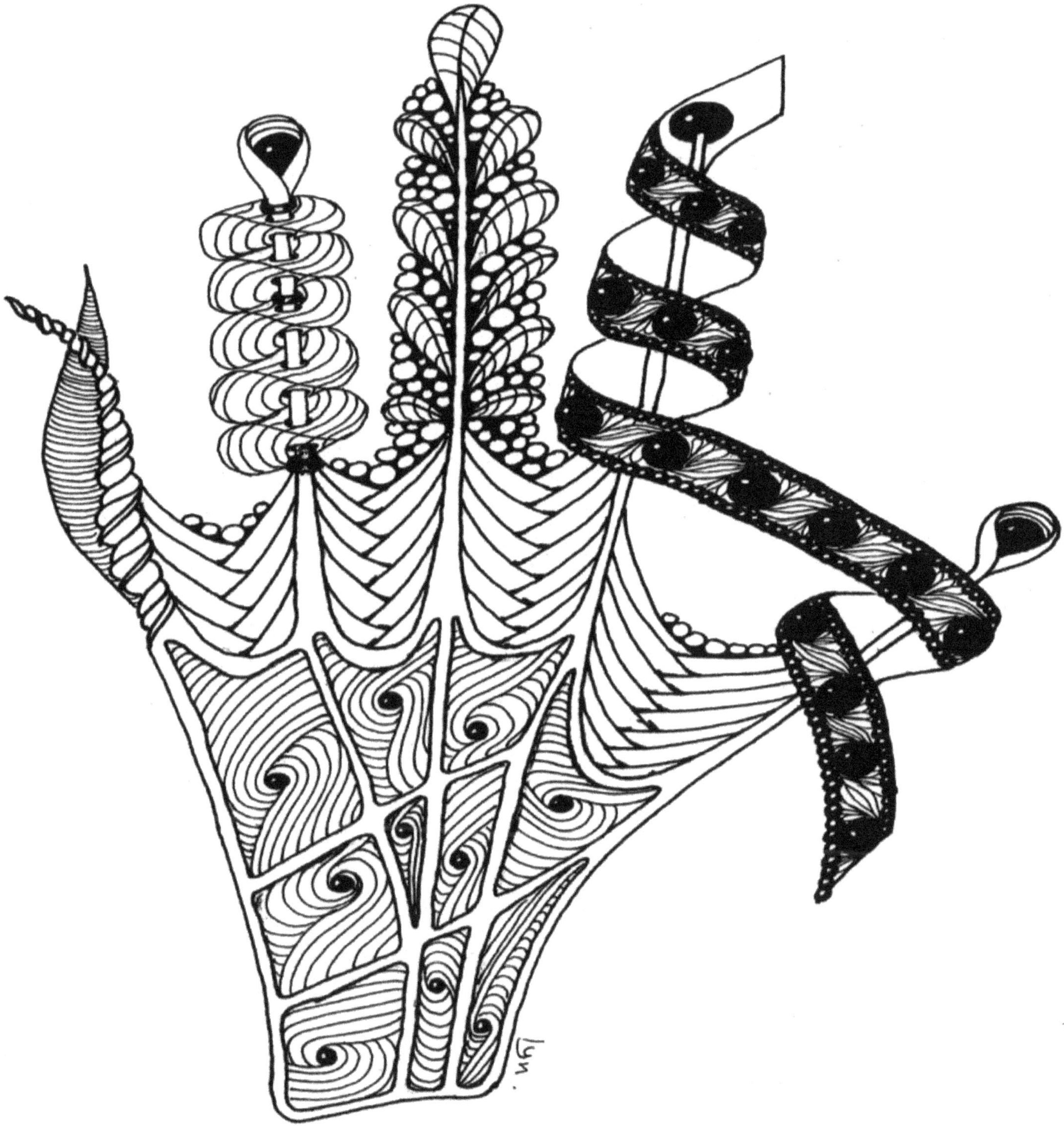

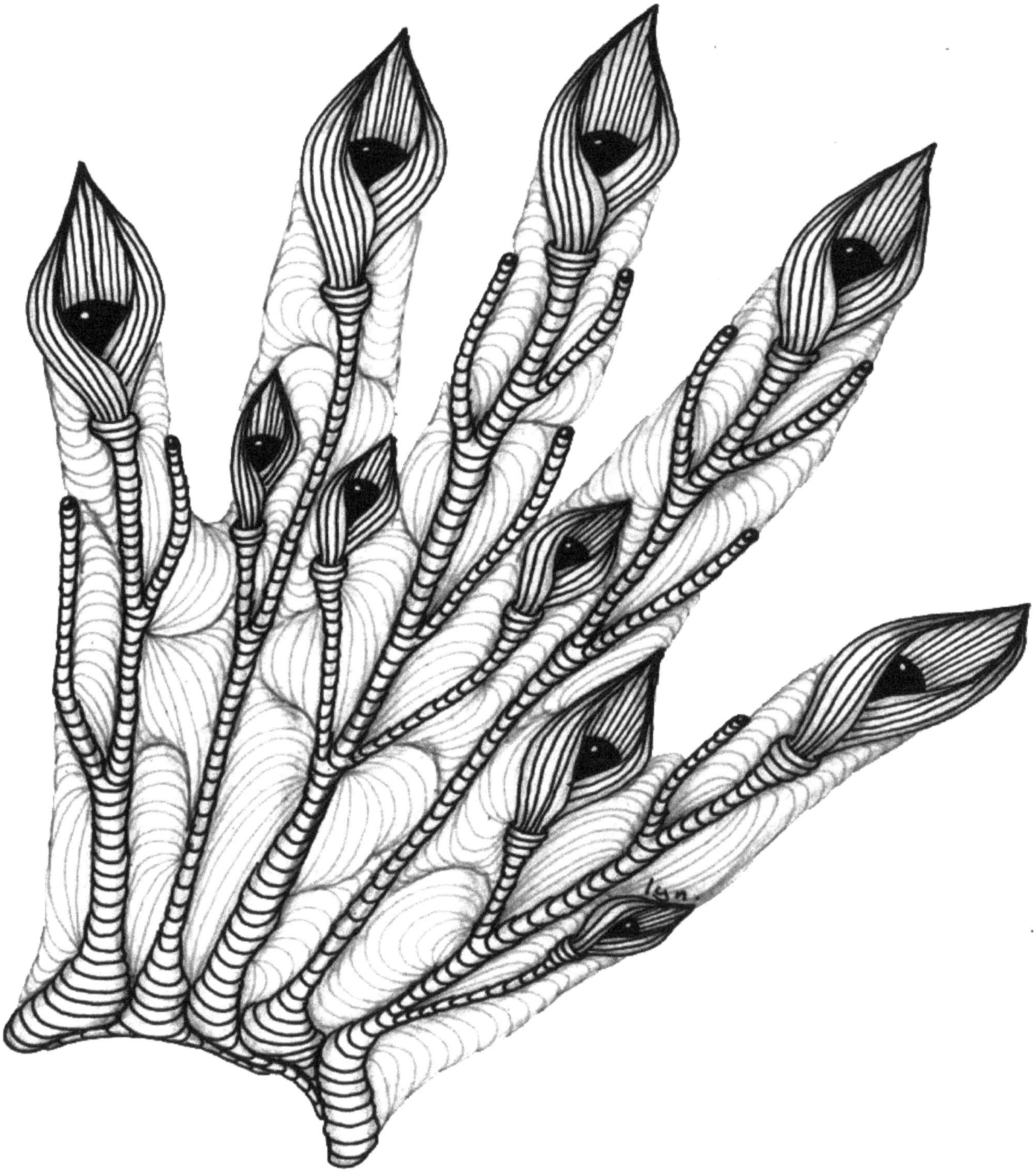

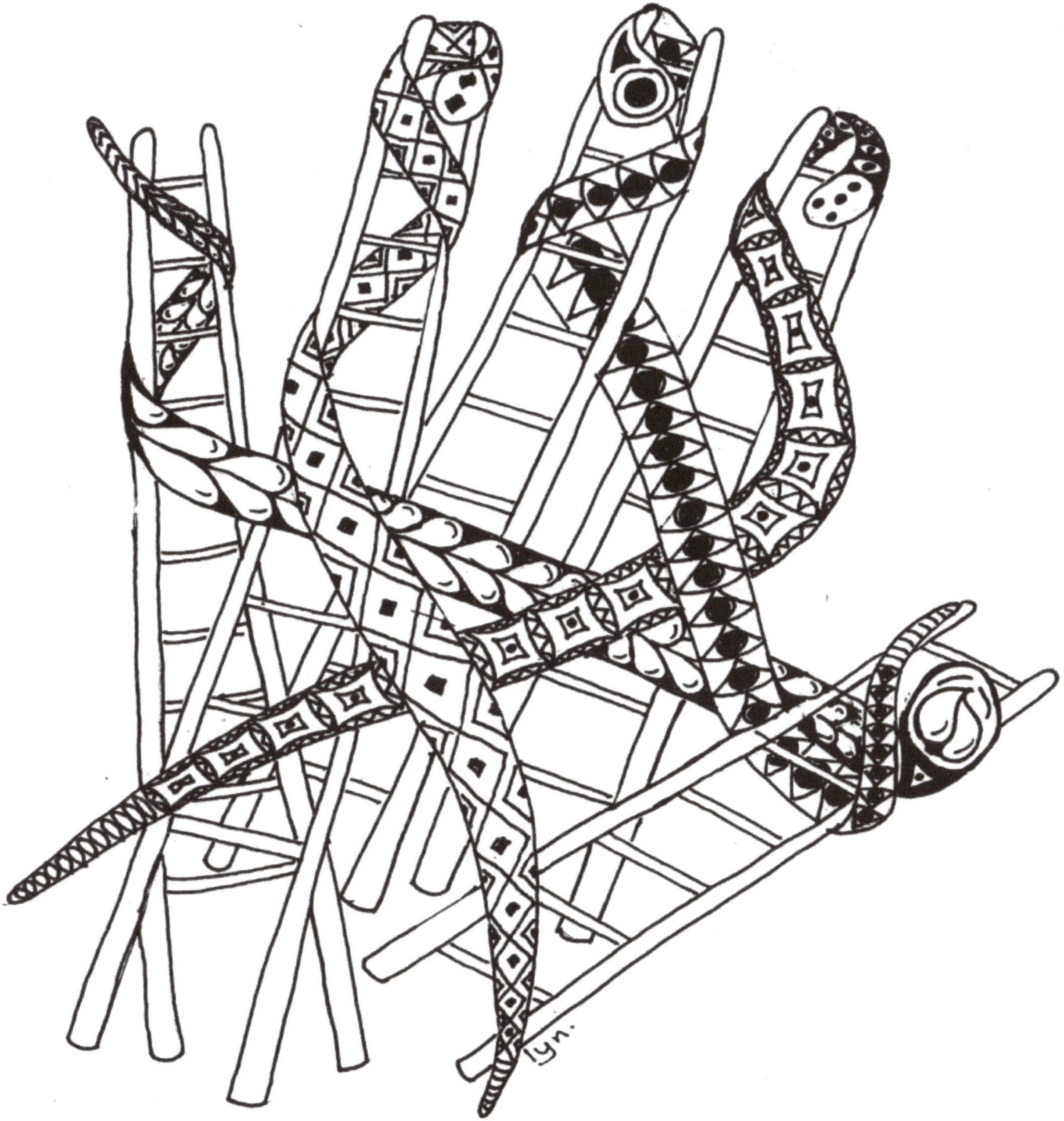
lyn.

www.ingramcontent.com/pod-product-compliance
Lightning Source LLC
Chambersburg PA
CBHW041638040420
42449CB00022B/3500
9781908135810